Policy Perspectives from Promising
New Scholars in Complexity
Volume III

Policy Perspectives from Promising New Scholars in Complexity

Volume III

DR. LIZ JOHNSON
& DR. JOSEPH COCHRAN

EDITORS

Westphalia Press
An Imprint of the Policy Studies Organization
Washington, DC
2019

POLICY PERSPECTIVES FROM PROMISING NEW SCHOLARS IN COMPLEXITY
VOLUME III

Westphalia Press
An imprint of Policy Studies Organization
1527 New Hampshire Ave., NW
Washington, D.C. 20036
info@ipsonet.org

ISBN-10: 1-63391-863-7
ISBN-13: 978-1-63391-863-4

Cover and interior design by Jeffrey Barnes
jbarnesbook.design

Daniel Gutierrez-Sandoval, Executive Director
PSO and Westphalia Press

Updated material and comments on this edition
can be found at the Westphalia Press website:
www.westphaliapress.org

CONTENTS

INTRODUCTION

It is important to remember that politics effectively becomes policy. Without research into the potential consequences of polarized political parties, without evaluation of the effectiveness of those continuing resolutions, it becomes the responsibility of researchers, academics, corporate leaders, and nonprofit workers, to determine whether these policies are benefiting the residents of the United States or if they are only benefiting the wealthy, who are usually capable of paying accountants and lawyers to take advantage of governmental decisions. In many ways, it is a thankless job to be a researcher in policy in the contemporary era, as the majority of the citizens within the system do not want to be reminded that they have limited guidance, as the majority of elected officials often do not want to be held accountable for not doing their jobs, and as the majority of the people outside of the system who benefit from the resulting chaos do not want the party to end. Regardless of whether anyone appreciates their services though, it is the responsibility of researchers to conduct their studies and report their results.

When it comes to the topic of complexity, things become even more confusing because people want simple answers and simple solutions, but the majority of questions that researchers pose do not have simple answers and the majority of problems faced by society do not have simple solution. In the environment that contemporary researchers face, simple answers are to be distrusted as they are often disguised propaganda and simple solutions are to be avoided as they are often confidence games. It is even worse when simple answers and simple solutions are found though, as the reason why the simple answers have been ignored is that they challenge the dogmas of the followers of the ruling political party and the reasons why the simple solutions have been avoided is that they threated the earnings of the allies of the ruling political party. In those cases, researchers who unwittingly reveal simple answers will be hounded by the followers of the ruling political party and who unassumingly propose simple solutions will be attacked by the allies of the ruling political party.

While that may make the entire situation seem untenable to researchers, this too shall pass and, as they say in statistics, regressions over time return to the mean. It is not to say that researchers should not be careful, online harassment can drive individuals to suicide and political attacks can ruin budding careers, but that they should be prepared for when policy stops being about politics. When that time comes again, and it will come through hook or crook, they will then be in a better position to publish their answers and to propose their solutions than the people who took advantage of the situation when politics became policy.

While it is in its formative phase, complexity science offers a new horizon for social science research because of people will desire accurate answers and proven solutions when policy stops being held hostage by politics. The insanity of contemporary politics will likely cause a backlash that will cause the general public to yearn for the stability of the scientific method. When the general public becomes fatigued by anger and tired of confrontation, it will be up to researchers, especially researchers who practice complexity science, to give them calm and thoughtful guidance. In order to do that though, practitioners of complexity science must not give up on their discipline and must endure until things change.

In the third book of this series, Policy Perspectives from Promising New Scholars in Complexity, we present a variety of research from scholars, the majority of whom are undergraduate through doctoral students, who have taken up the challenge of integrating complexity science into their work. In some cases, the scholars present finished research. In other cases, the scholars present aspirational research. It is our hope that the work of our contributors will inspire other researchers to continue their work in using complexity science in relation to public policy and will encourage other researchers to endure through the darkness that will be coming before the dawn.

ECONOMIC
POLICY

THE NEW WAVE OF FOREIGN COMPETITION

Deepak Mirchandani

INTRODUCTION

Have you purchased an item from Amazon prime recently? If you have, according to Forbes, there is a good chance that your purchase can have an extremely negative impact on U.S. Small Businesses (Shepard, 2017b). Today, you are going to learn about "The New Wave of Foreign Competition." There is a significant number of Chinese-based sellers, selling directly to the consumer here in the United States (Shepard, 2017a) and it's killing American businesses. All this is happening in the background, and the consumer has no idea where the company that they are purchasing from is based. My point of view is an employee of an American-owned small business and a student at the University of North Carolina at Charlotte. The goal of this paper is to inform Americans of the impacts of direct foreign competition on the U.S. economy and challenge the current policies to solve this problem in a way that would benefit all parties involved.

You may be thinking in your mind that my products are made in China anyways. So, why does this even matter? Well, the difference is now more of the profits are going to China. What does that mean? For example, let's say there is an American company selling an iPhone case online. They manufacture the case for $2 USD in China, and they sell it for $10 to you the consumer in the United States. Now the factory in China sees the opportunity to sell that iPhone case directly to you, so they send to one of Amazon's fulfillment centers here in America and sell the same product for $9.50. So, before when you were buying that case, $2 was going to China, and $8 was going back in the domestic economy. As the consumer is searching for an iPhone case on Amazon, there is no indication that the item is being sold by an American seller or a foreign one. This is a very surface level example of the problem that American small businesses are trying to develop a solution to.

THE IMPACT OF FOREIGN TRADE

How much is foreign direct retailing impacting American businesses and the U.S. economy? There is not much research done on this topic, and I was not able to find much information. However, I did find out that locations of some Amazon Marketplace Sellers are released to Amazon business buyers. So, I used a family member's EIN and signed up for an Amazon Business Account. Amazon also publishes the top 100 selling items per category to the public. So, together I could combine the data from these two places and find out just how successful these sellers are on Amazon. So, I went through the top 100 selling products in a few categories and filtered the top 10 products that were sold by marketplace sellers and counted the number of Chinese sellers within this filter. Note that this data was collected on November 30, 2017, and it's, possible that it could have changed since then. The results were fascinating. In the "Clothing" category, six out of the ten were Chinese sellers. The other four items consisted of branded goods, such as "Wrangler Jeans" which are hard to imitate. In the "Industrial and Scientific," category five out of the 10 items were sold by the Chinese. In the "Luggage and Travel Gear" had eight out of the 10, "Musical Instruments" had five out of the 10, "Tools and Home Improvement" had four out of the 10, and the last category that I reviewed was "Beauty and Personal Care" which had three out of the 10 as direct Chinese sellers. Almost all the Chinese companies were sending their merchandise to Amazon's American fulfillment centers and qualifying for "Amazon Prime." Which means that the customer does not have to wait for weeks to get their order from abroad, they can have it within two business days according to Amazon. com (Amazon, 2018).

Foreign competition happens all around us, and we see it every single day. As you are driving down the road, it is very likely that you see an Exxon gas station right beside a Shell gas station. Exxon is American-based, whereas Shell is Dutch-based. Or even Apple versus Samsung, Apple is American, whereas Samsung is South Korea. It's happening all around us, and it is challenging American companies to continue and innovate. However, the "New wave of foreign competition" is very different and provides foreign sellers with unfair advantages over U.S.-based companies. So, what are these advantages? Let's start with the workforce. In a study conducted by China Daily calculating China highest minimum wage, they found that Beijing has the highest in the nation where workers get paid $2.90 per hour (Xinhua, 2015, p. 1). Whereas CNN figured the median hourly wage of a warehouse worker in the United States is around $13.50 (Fox, 2013, p. 1). More than four times more expensive compared to China. According to the Internal Revenue Service, if a foreign company has U.S. physical presence, they are liable to pay American income tax. However, if the foreign corporation has no physical presence here in America, then they will not have to pay any income tax here in the United States (IRS Publication 54, 2018, p. 1).

Since Chinese sellers are just sending their items to Amazon's fulfillment centers, they are avoiding their own company's physical presence and having the advantage of having their item shipped from the US to the customer. Because of this, in most cases, they do not have to pay income taxes here in America (IRS Publication 54, 2018, p. 1). Since the Chinese companies are not based in a state, they also avoid charging and paying sales tax here in the United States in most cases. Chinese sellers also have a huge advantage when they are shipping small packaged items to the west.

According to a study by Fortune, China is considered an undeveloped country in the eyes of the United Nations and is getting postal services subsidized by the arriving nation (Morris, 2015). Morris gives the example of a voice recording component being sold by a Chinese seller on eBay for $1.96 and free shipping from China, whereas the same item is being sold for $9.99 plus $6.99 shipping from Radio Shack. Morris explains that the cost of shipping from China to the United States is significantly cheaper than sending an item domestically here in the United States. Also, according to contributors on Amazon seller forums, Chinese sellers are also obtaining other advantages over U.S. sellers. Such as avoiding import duties on items being sent to the United States. One contributor even highlights how he is unable to sell on Amazon China when Chinese sellers can sell on Amazon US anytime. These items from the forums are not easily proven. However, they do sound realistic.

Is there any difference between an item sold by an American seller compared to a foreign one? Regarding speed, since foreign sellers are using services such as "Fulfillment by Amazon," the delivery speed is almost always the same compared to an individual small business mailing the item out to you. Regarding quality, since most of the items are made in China anyway, the Chinese factories already know the quality that

American consumers are wanting, so there is virtually no difference. Regarding cost, Chinese sellers can usually sell the item significantly cheaper due to the advantages that they have. For authenticity, CNBC concludes that there are many Chinese sellers selling counterfeit goods (Levy, 2016). However, marketplaces like Amazon are becoming experts at detecting this. Lastly, regarding overall experience, I would argue that the overall experience of buying an item from a U.S. seller to is very similar overall. All of this is happening before our eyes without the consumer knowing about it.

Forbes did a case study on a company called Boredwalk created by a man named Matthew Snow. In 2014, he had an idea to create t-shirts with humorous designs on them (Shepard, 2017a). He started selling his shirts on Etsy.com. Snow was extremely successful with them and was formally invited to join Amazon's marketplace. Sales began to take off after he started selling on Amazon. However, shortly after by the end of 2015, he saw a huge decline in sales. He did some investigations and found out that several Chinese sellers were counterfeiting his item and selling it as his. After lengthy disputes with Amazon, he was unable to remove the Chinese sellers off his company's listings. So, eventually he ordered that Amazon remove everything with his company's brand name. Snow claims that his company lost a lot of money. This is just a small example of what can happen to a significant portion of American businesses operating on Amazon and other similar marketplaces.

Overall, this benefits the consumers. The customers get to enjoy extremely low prices on many top essentials and general items. However, I would argue that these benefits are not going to be long-term benefits. Since these Chinese companies have the price advantage and power to kill competition over time they can increase prices. I would also argue that several of the consumers purchasing the items are putting their future jobs at stake. Because there is a growing population of people working for online businesses and if unfair foreign competition is removing these companies then those jobs will no longer exist here in America.

CONCLUSION

Unfair foreign competition can be utterly disastrous for U.S. small businesses and the American economy overall. However, we need to be able to develop solutions that can protect local businesses from this new wave of unfair competition. There are several different approaches to the problem. For example, we could require that each small package entering the United States be subject to import duties. Currently, only packages over $800 and gifts over $100 are subject to import duties. This will help local companies by driving the cost of foreign goods up and potentially increasing the turnaround time for packages providing U.S. companies with an advantage. Another possible solution could be to require organizations such as Amazon and eBay to ensure that their sellers are competing fairly by verifying all rules and regulations are being followed. Lastly, online marketplaces must require that the location of the business selling on the platform to be visible to the public. This measure will allow consumers to decide if they want to spend more to protect local jobs and businesses. Several solutions can be implemented; these three are just examples. However, we need to come together and develop a method that would keep our small businesses strong and our economy thriving.

Thank you for your time!

REFERENCES

Amazon (2018). *Prime delivery*. Retrieve from https://www.amazon.com/b?ie=UTF8&node=15247183011

Fox, E.J. (2013, July 30). How Amazon's new jobs really stack up. CNN Business. Retrieved from https://money.cnn.com/2013/07/30/news/companies/amazon-warehouse-workers/index.html.

IRS (2018). *Taxation of nonresident aliens*. Retrieved from https://www.irs.gov/individuals/international-taxpayers/taxation-of-nonresident-aliens

Levy, A. (2016, July 8). Amazon's Chinese counterfeit problem is getting worse. CNBC. Retrieved from https://www.cnbc.com/2016/07/08/amazons-chinese-counterfeit-problem-is-getting-worse.html.

Morris, D.Z. (2015, March 11). The United Nations is helping subsidize

Chinese shipping. Here's how. *Fortune*. Retrieved from http://fortune. com/2015/03/11/united-nations-subsidy-chinese-shipping/

Shepard, W. (2017a, March 17). How Amazon's wooing of Chinese sellers is killing small American businesses. *Forbes*. Retrieved from https://www.forbes.com/sites/wadeshepard/2017/02/14/how-amazons-wooing-of-chinese-sellers-is-hurting-american-innovation/#5cc6aec1df25

Shepard, W. (2017b, October 01). Amazon.com: The place where American dreams are stolen by Chinese counterfeiters. *Forbes*. Retrieved from https://www.forbes.com/sites/wadeshepard/2017/09/27/amazon-com-the-place-where-american-dreams-are-stolen-by-chinese-counterfeiters/#117b158c4c72

Xinhua. (2015, September 30). Beijing tops China's hourly minimum wage. *China Daily*. Retrieved from http://www.chinadaily.com.cn/china/2015-09/30/content_22017853.htm

ENERGY
POLICY

A CRITICAL EXAMINATION OF HYDRAULIC FRACTURING

Hunter Healy

INTRODUCTION

Hydraulic fracturing, commonly referred to as "fracking," is the process of injecting water, sand, and chemicals at a high pressure, deep into the ground, to fracture, or split open, rock formation. Doing so releases natural gas, a form of energy that can be used to generate electricity, fuel cars, heat homes, and more! The mechanical engineering practices used in fracturing date back to the 1860s, when the practice of shooting gunpowder down a well with what is described as an "exploding torpedo," was patented by Edward Roberts (Manfreda, 2015). Water's suitable use for fracturing would not be discovered until the 1900s, when history experienced the birth of fracking.

THE SCIENCE OF FRACKING

That which is known as fracking has evolved significantly over the past 75 years, with natural gas now accounting for roughly 28 percent of the United States' yearly energy consumption, according to the Energy Information Administration (EIA, 2018). However, fracking does not come without controversy. While its economic and, in some instances, social benefit cannot be ignored, fracking is a harmful practice largely due to its environmental effects and the risk it poses to water security (Stone, 2017).

Fracking is an intricate operation that is closely tied to the study of geology and it is first important to understand how the process takes place. Natural gas is a fossil fuel, meaning it derives from organisms that existed during the Carboniferous Period, during the Paleozoic Era (Batema, 2017). Over time, as plants and animals died, their remains, also known as biomass, were covered under many layers of material such as sand and clay. The dead plants and trees were placed under immense pressure and heat as the sedimentary layers of rock formed above.

Eventually, moisture trapped within the innermost layers of organic material was released, forming natural gas (Union of Concerned Scientists, 2015). This chemical process can be explained as the breaking down of carbon bonds. Fittingly, the main ingredient in natural gas is methane, an extremely flammable gas with the chemical formula, CH_4, which is a combination of the elements Carbon and Hydrogen. Of the two types of natural gas, dry and wet, dry natural gas is most preferred by consumers due to its high concentration of methane which makes it more conducive to regular-usage settings.

As discussed, natural gas forms in environments where prehistoric plant and occasionally animal organisms once lived. Across impermeable rock layers, where said fossils exist, porous, natural gas reservoirs have developed. Perhaps as early as 6,000 BCE, the first natural gas sites were discovered by prehistoric inhabitants of Iran (Dyck, 2017). The Middle East is an environment where one is likely to find natural gas reservoirs.

According to the 2012 Statistical Review of World Energy conducted by BP, 10 middle-eastern countries comprising roughly only 3.5 percent of the land on Earth account for 38 percent of natural gas reserves (BP, 2012, p. 20). According to geologist Rasoul Sorkhabi (2011), a thriving history of sedimentation along the portion of the Gondwana supercontinent on which the Middle East is located today could explain this disproportionate concentration of natural gas resources. It is also believed that the diversity of the oceanic microorganisms that developed in this area contributed to the superfluity of natural gas in this location. It was just a matter of being at the right place, at the right time, over the course of the Earth's history!

THE PROCESS OF FRACKING

Fracking is the process of extracting natural gas through the process of drilling underground wells and then using water pressure to fracture the underlying shale formations; however, in practice, it is much more complex (Lallanilla, 2018). The first step in the fracturing process is for the temporary drilling rig, also known as a derrick, to be built. Drilling usually occurs at minimum, 5,000 feet below the water table, where the aquifers that supply fresh drinking water are located. Surface casing, which is usually constructed out of steel piping, is inserted vertically, into the ground. The purpose of surface casing is to ensure that no natural gas interacts with any potential underground sources of drinking water, thus preventing contamination. Additionally, more metal pipes, known as conductor casings, are inserted and cemented in place to further prevent any gas from escaping. The vertical drilling stops at about 500 feet before the location of natural gas and then horizontal drilling begins. Horizontal drilling can extend underground for up to nearly two miles. Next, what is known as perforating occurs. A perforating gun is inserted into the well and an assortment of tiny holes are created that enable the contents of the shale layer to enter the wellbore, or drilling hole, casing, and vice versa. Finally, the drilling equipment is removed, and a well head caps the wellbore at Earth's surface.

However, what makes *hydraulic* fracturing effective is that after perforating occurs, fracking solution containing a plethora of strategically designed chemicals, is pumped down and through the perforated holes at immensely high pressures, further breaking apart the shale formation. Sand that acts as a proppant is then pumped into the shale formation as well, to keep it from closing and preventing natural gas from entering back into the pipe. All this, allowing for the natural gas reservoir to be released and continue to the surface, along with the initial substance injected that the Environmental Protection Agency describes as "flowback liquid" (EPA, n.d.)

The sophisticated process of fracking has evolved a great deal over the years since the time of "exploding torpedoes" being shot down into the Earth. In 1949, Halliburton was one of the first private sector companies to employ fracturing for commercial use (Wells, n.d.). With the principal concept now in place, chemical engineers are now refining fracking solution and seismologists are working to more precisely locate areas of potential natural gas reservoirs. Perhaps, the most valuable advancement in fracking technology has been the development of durable, impermeable casings to prevent methane from directly crossing the water table, thus protecting underground water resources and the safety of the public.

Still yet, fracking is expensive. Schlumberger Ltd. and Halliburton Co. are two of the largest energy conglomerates in the world, invested in the fracking industry. Even North Carolina's own, Duke Energy, has its foot in the fracking business. Fracking efforts remain largely in the private sector, as does funding. However, it's worth noting that the government has given significant tax-breaks to companies pursuing "unconventional drilling." Reports also show that the U.S. Department of Energy has sponsored fracking research studies (Office of Fossil Energy, n.d.).

THE UTILITY OF FRACKING

I do not support fracking due to its harmful environmental impacts and its nominal social and economic benefits. According to Cohen (2011), in the decades leading up to 2011, energy companies spent hundreds of millions of dollars lobbying U.S. federal lawmakers to support fracking. While this statistic suggests that there is great economic incentive in fracking, more recently, as of 2016, projections show that more than half the nation's fracking industry could go out of business if the price of oil continues to fall to historic lows; the price of a barrel of oil in January was just around $30 dollars (Gross, 2017). According to the Brookings Institute, the price of natural gas decreased by 47 percent in 2013, due to the dramatic boom in fracking operations (Hausman & Kellogg, 2015). Still, even with this in consideration, natural gas is becoming obsolete in relation to its more affordable, and less controversial counterpart.

If the social goal of the fracking industry (if there ever was one!) is to create greater access to energy, in doing so, the hydraulic fracturing companies have neglected to consider the ways in which the fracking industry has impacted people's lives (Jameel, 2016). While it's true, fracking creates jobs, so does the Mafia. When wells are drilled, frequently in rural communities, the geographic landscape of the town is altered and supporting infrastructure often must be constructed. Not only can this pose a significant threat to surrounding ecosystems, it can also pose dangerous health risks to the residents as well. As reported in the Gasland documentary (Adiesic, Gandour, Fox, Roma, & Fox, 2010), a homeowner in a small Dakota town at the center of the fracking revolution reported that his tap-water ignited in flames while he was brushing his teeth in 2013. If one will recall, methane, the main ingredient in natural gas, is highly flammable. Perhaps, the fracking companies' surface and conductor casings are not as reliable a barrier as initially thought. Or more likely, perhaps the companies are improperly disposing of "flowback liquid," as significant contributor to the harsh environmental effects of fracking.

There are regulatory frameworks with specific guidelines set in place by the Environmental Protection Agency to ensure proper disposal of this substance, with most it being placed in underground injection wells monitored by the EPA. However, too often, there are incidences where companies are held with little to no accountability (McKenna, 2015). Additionally, a major threat that poses is the unknown. The long-term environmental implications of fracking are unbeknownst to anyone. Alarmingly, the ingredients in fracking fluid used by major companies are classified as trade-secrets. Essentially, what we are placing in the ground and what is potentially contaminating our drinking water is being kept secret for the sole purpose of protecting a laissez-faire economic culture. It is sensible that we should not sacrifice our biological health (along with ecological and environmental), for the sake of allowing big companies to make profit. Several states have issued fracking disclosure legislation; however, the overwhelming majority have not.

CONCLUSION

Fracking is a harmful practice that should not continue. We must direct our resources to solar and wind energy, both of which pose a significantly lesser risk to our planet and our health. Water is a limited resource that is being jeopardized, even without the presence of the fracking industry. Less than 1 percent of all water on Earth is easily accessible freshwater, and it is recommended that each of the over seven billion people on our planet drink two quarts of it per day. We *need* water to sustain life, and it comes with no alternative. Conversely, energy has over five alternative renewable sources already known to man; hence, it does not necessitate the process of fracking.

REFERENCES

Adiesic, T., Gandour, M., Fox, J., Roma, D. (Producers), & Fox, J. (Director). (2010). *Gasland* [Motion Picture]. USA: New Video Group/HBO/International WOW Company.

Batema, C. (2017, April 25). Elements in fossil fuels. *Sciencing*. Retrieved from https://sciencing.com/elements-fossil-fuels-7166.html

BP (2012). BP statistical review of world energy, June 2012. Retrieved from https://www.bp.com/content/dam/bp-country/de_at/pdfs/20120620_statistical_review_of_world_energy_full_report_2012.pdf

Cohen, R. (2011, November 15). Campaign and lobbying expenditures promote fracking big time. *Nonprofit Quarterly*. Retrieved from https://nonprofitquarterly.org/2011/11/15/campaign-and-lobbying-expenditures-promote-fracking-big-time/

Dyck, S. (2017, August 15). Did you know: natural gas. *Hard Hat Hunter*. Retrieved from https://blog.hardhathunter.com/know-natural-gas/

EIA (2018). *Primary energy consumption estimates by source.* Retrieved from https://www.eia.gov/totalenergy/data/annual/index.php

EPA (n.d.). *The process of unconventional natural gas production.* Retrieved from https://www.epa.gov/uog/process-unconventional-natural-gas-production

Gross, S. (2017, October 19). The new energy abundance-what happens when energy prices are lower for longer. *Brookings*. Retrieved from https://www.brookings.edu/blog/order-from-chaos/2017/10/19/the-new-energy-abundance-what-happens-when-energy-prices-are-lower-for-longer/

Hausman, C. & Kellogg, R. (2015). Welfare and distribution implications of shale gas. *Brookings*. Retrieved from https://www.brookings.edu/bpea-articles/welfare-and-distributional-implications-of-shale-gas/

Jameel, M. (2016, June 23). Rural Pennsylvanians say fracking "just ruined everything." *Huffpost*. Retrieved from https://www.huffingtonpost.com/entry/pennsylvania-fracking-water_us_576b7a76e4b0c0252e786d5e

Lallanilla, M. (2018, February 9). Facts about fracking. *Live Science*. Retrieved from https://www.livescience.com/34464-what-is-fracking.html

Manfreda, J. (2015, April 13). The real history of fracking. *OilPrice.com*.

Retrieved from https://oilprice.com/Energy/Crude-Oil/The-Real-History-Of-Fracking.html

McKenna, P. (2015, August 26). Environmental groups start the process to sue EPA over fracking waste. *Inside Climate News*. Retrieved from https://insideclimatenews.org/news/26082015/environmental-groups-start-legal-process-sue-epa-over-fracking-waste-wastewater

Office of Fossil Energy (n.d.). Shale research & development. *Energy.gov*. Retrieved from https://www.energy.gov/fe/science-innovation/oil-gas-research/shale-gas-rd

Sorkhabi, R. (2011). Finding Ghawar: elephant hid in desert. *AAPG Explorer*. Retrieved from http://archives.aapg.org/explorer/2011/06jun/ghawar0611.cfm

Stone, J. (2017, February 23). Fracking is dangerous to your health—here's why. *Forbes*. Retrieved from https://www.forbes.com/sites/judystone/2017/02/23/fracking-is-dangerous-to-your-health-heres-why/#4363db6e5945

Union of Concerned Scientists (2015, April 3). *How natural gas is formed*. Retrieve from

https://www.ucsusa.org/clean-energy/coal-and-other-fossil-fuels/how-is-natural-gas-formed

Wells, B.A. (n.d.). Shooters–a "fracking" history. *American Oil & Gas Historical Society*. Retrieved from https://aoghs.org/technology/hydraulic-fracturing/

JUSTICE
POLICY

COMPLEXITY AND POLICE ACCOUNTABILITY

Dr. Joseph Cochran

INTRODUCTION

In recent years, American society has been faced with the uncomfortable realization that minorities, suspects, and women have been illtreated by local polices officers. It has been forced to acknowledge that there are police officers who have been raping women by the side of the road after pulling them over during for traffic stops (Gerber, 2018). It has also been forced to acknowledge that there are police officer have been shooting minority suspects because they distrust and fear the members of minority communities rather than because of the actions of minority suspects (Wallace-Wells, 2016).

What allows police to think that they can get away with assaulting women? It comes from a lack of accountability of the police by the leaders of their communities and an inherent trust by law bidding citizens in United States in the rightness of the actions of the police. Police officers are often portrayed in the entertainment media as heroic characters, with rogue cops being shown as mavericks who bend or break the law to pursue justice, which bad or corrupt cops usually being portrayed primarily as adversaries of other police officers rather than primarily as threats to local communities (Donovan & Klahm, 2015). According to Donovan and Klahm (2015), police procedurals, rather than personal interactions with the police or new reports about police misconduct, shape many of the public opinions concerning police officers and, since police officers are protagonists within such television shows, they often show police officers in a positive light.

What has caused the distrust and fear of minorities among police? Is it because policing is a terribly dangerous job? No, not really, police officers are not even among the top ten professions in fatality rates (Fleetwood, 2015). One possible source of the problem may be more about the perception of danger than the reality of danger which, once again, could possibly be traced to media, which often portrays minorities as criminals (Punyanunt-Carter, 2008). Another possible source of the problem though could be institutional racism within police forces, which may allow police officers to commit brutalities against members of minority communities without fear of consequences (Cheney & Robertson, 2013).

In any case, misbehavior of police officers can be attributed to a lack of police accountability. Police officers are human beings, and some human being misbehave if they know that they will not face consequences from their actions, which is really the entire reason why societies have criminal justice systems. Complexity models may help communities improve police accountability by allowing them to detect actions that are often indicators of criminal police behavior and to investigate suspicious police officers before they critically harm local communities.

POLICE ACCOUNTABILITY

What do we mean by police accountability? First, it means that police officers have professional training in the criminal justice field and are not just repurposed military personnel or untrained civilian vigilantes. Second, it means that police officers are answerable to the courts of law and to independent review boards that monitor their interactions with the local community. Third, it means that police are willing to report any questionable activities by their fellow officers and that residents are willing to report any crimes that they witness committed by police officers. Essentially, it means that police officers (and the communities that they serve) benefit from accountability, oversight, and integrity (UNODC, 2011).

Professional training is important to police accountability because it allows police officers understand the limits of their legal authority and what degree of force is appropriate while pursuing their duties (Klinger, 2012). While MPs (Military Police) possess professional training, their training focuses on the application of military law, not civilian law, so they would not be considered adequate substitutes for civilian police without additional training. In many jurisdictions, security guards require certification and training, but they lack law enforcement powers because they have not gone through the specialized training of police officers.

Within the United States, police officers are given great discretionary powers when it comes to arresting an individual and when it comes to using lethal force. While the legality of individual actions might seem without question to a civilian observer, it is up to police officers to determine whether they should let an individual off with a citation or a warning, or if they should arrest an individual. When it comes to the use of lethal force, the automatic assumption in the criminal justice system is that police officers are justified in the use of lethal force unless there is contradicting evidence. It is only through monitoring the police that residents can know that the police are acting within the law (Muth & Jack, 2016).

While most police officers in the United States are dedicated professionals who honorably perform their duties, there are notable exceptions. Bad cops, either corrupt cops who use their position of authority to receive material benefits (drugs, money, sexual favors, etc.) or rogue cops who use excessive force regardless of the situation, endanger the lives of good cops by decreasing the public trust in police officers, which is why good cops and concerned residents should report questionable activities by other cops. Unfortunately, police officers tend to protect their own, so every resident of a community should feel obligated to report questionable activities by police officers to maintain the public trust. The federal government maintains the Civil Rights Division of the Department of Justice to deal with any cases of reported local police misconduct (Civil Rights Division, 2015).

Public trust is an essential aspect of modern policing in the United States because there are more than 400 residents for every police officer (U.S. Department of Justice, 2015). In effect, policing becomes quite difficult if the residents of a community decide not to cooperate with the local police. If the local community trusts its police officers, its residents will come forward to report criminal activities that the local police force might be unaware of, allowing police officers to deal with criminals before they do excessive harm to the community. If the local community does not trust its police officers though, its residents will start to see the local police force as outsiders who are there to victimize their neighbors, which allows criminals to continue to harm the local community through any variety of criminal activities.

Public trust in the local police force also influences the willingness of suspects to submit to being arrested rather than just opening fire when police officers come around. If suspects feel that the local police force is honest, then they will probably submit to arrest even if they have committed a crime because they will feel that they will have a chance to justify (or obfuscate) their actions before a jury of their peers. If suspects feel that the local police force is dishonest however, then they will probably not submit to arrest even if they have not committed a crime because they will feel like they will not have a chance to prove their innocence within the court system. In nations with corrupt police forces, the lack of public trust means that the residents of those nations view the entire justice system with skepticism, as they understand that their individual power and wealth governs the justice that they receive (Bayley & Perito, 2011).

KEEPING POLICE ACCOUNTABLE

There are several methods through which police officers can be kept accountable. They are held accountable by their fellow police officers, the local communities, and by the authorities. These methods of accountability include Peer Accountability, Community Surveillance, Internal Affairs, Citizen Review Boards, Prosecutorial Discretion, State and Federal Investigations, and Civil Lawsuits and Criminal Charges.

Most of the police officers seem to be held accountable, informally or formally, by other police before they become a problem (Quinn, 2017). While the "blue shield" does exist in some police forces, it is the responsibility of police officers to enforce the law, regardless of who is breaking the law. In the case of informal accountability, senior police officers keep track of the activities of junior police officers to make sure that they are stable enough and honest enough to wear the uniform and, if not, pressure them to leave the profession. In the case of formal accountability, the superiors of police officers are given wide latitude on assignments and punishments for police officers who cause problems, up to and including demotions in rank and assignment to undesirable duties.

With the advent of video cameras, especially video cameras on cell phones, the residents of a community are capable of recording police activities with unprecedented accuracy (Krupanski, 2012). While there have always been reports of certain police officers mistreating suspects, it was historically difficult for the residents of a community to prove mistreatment unless their stories were corroborated by people who possessed authority, meaning that the mistreatment would often continue until the tensions in the local community had reached a tipping point (Joseph, 2016). With video cameras, however, residents of a community can hold police accountable by providing evidence of misdeeds. Community surveillance is becoming an important part of proving the use of excessive force against suspects (or just innocent bystanders), though there are efforts by police forces and local authorities to restrict community surveillance (Balko, 2010).

In most larger police forces, Internal Affairs (IA) departments exist to investigate potential misconduct by police officers (COPS, 2007). Larger police forces will also maintain a Firearms Discharge Review Board (FDRB) or similar board to review every incident where a police officer fired a lethal round from a weapon outside of hunting and similar activities (Rose, 2013). If IA becomes involved, it usually means that peer accountability has failed to address a problematic police officer, and, in recent years, it may mean that community surveillance has succeeded in catching a police officer doing questionable actions. If IA discovers maleficence on behalf of a police officer, it can recommend anything from a formal reprimand to dismissal to felony charges against the police officer.

Civilian review boards (CRBs) are independent boards appointed by local civilian authorities that examine reports of inappropriate behavior by police officers (Finn, 2001). Since they are created by local civilian authorities to oversee local police forces, they tend to vary widely in their authority and their mission. In general, they tend to be divided into three types: Investigative CRBs that independently investigate inappropriate behavior by police officers, Review CRBs that independently review the findings of police forces on the suspected inappropriate behavior by police officers, and Auditing CRBs that independently audit the internal review process of police forces.

Prosecutors have a subtle way of enforcing police accountability by deciding whether to indict suspects who have been arrested for a crime (Zeidman, 2005). While prosecutors will rarely fail to indict suspects that were arrested during the commission of a crime unless the police officers involved were engaged in maleficence during the arrest, they are much less likely to indict suspects if they know that the arresting officer is under suspicion for inappropriate behavior. Prosecutors tend to be evaluated by their successful convictions, and they tend not to want to have their cases thrown out due to police officers engaging in inappropriate behavior or to have their cases that resulted in convictions overturned because police officers engaged in maleficence (Nugent-Borakove & Budzilowicz, 2007).

When everything fails at the local level to address problems with police accountability, that is generally when the state and/or federal authorities step in. State authorities tend to be more sympathetic to local police forces than federal authorities, so their investigations tend to focus on addressing immediate problems of police accountability and will tend to guide local police forces in fixing their problems (Norwood, 2017). Federal authorities tend to be less sympathetic to local police forces than state authorities, so their investigations tend to examine every potential case of police misconduct and will tend to force local police forces to restructure their policies and their training to make sure that the problems of police accountability are not repeated (Department of Justice, 2017).

How Society Deals with Local Police Misconduct

One example of how state authorities deal with local police misconduct can be found in California (Norwood, 2017). After decades of local governments being unable to take care of the misconduct of their police forces, California explicitly gave its attorney general the authority to oversee local police forces (making it the only state that gives its attorney generals that authority). In 1998, William Lockyer was the first attorney general to use that authority, eventually resulting in the reform of the Riverside Police Department in 2001. While other states lack such explicit authority for their attorney generals, most of them have more subtle methods of enforcing police accountability, such as issuing and revoking police licenses.

Unlike state authorities, federal authorities deal with local police misconduct when it violates the civil rights of citizens. In general, federal oversight of local police misconduct is the province of the Department of Justice (Police Executive Research Forum, 2013). The Department of Justice tends to get involved in six major areas: Police Use of Force,

Early Intervention Systems, Management and Supervision of Officers, Biased Policing and Unlawful Stops, Searches, and Arrests, Gender Bias in the Handling of Sexual Assaults, and Police Interaction with Persons with Mental Illness. The Department of Justice tends to use consent decrees to change the behavior of local police departments that it finds guilty of misconduct (Department of Justice, 2017).

CONSEQUENCES OF LOCAL POLICE MISCONDUCT

When everything is said and done, severe lapses in police accountability tend to result in civil lawsuits and/or criminal charges. In the case of civil lawsuits, the people who were harmed by maleficence on the part of police officers may sue police officers, police forces, and/or local governments for recompense (Schwartz, 2016). Civil lawsuits can be extraordinarily expensive for local municipalities, with some cities spending hundreds of millions of dollars to settle civil lawsuits and paying tens of millions of dollars in legal fees caused by police misconduct (Balko, 2014). In effect, everyone in a community pays for police misconduct due to the local municipalities having to reduce services and/or increase taxes to settle civil lawsuits and pay legal fees. In the case of criminal charges, police officers who engaged in inappropriate behavior, and any police officers who helped to conceal the inappropriate behavior, may face misdemeanor and/or felony charges, depending on the level of harm and the level of culpability of the individual in question (Bedi, 2017).

How often do police officers face prosecution? While most police officers avoid legal trouble, around 1,000 police officers end up being arrested every year (Ferner, 2016). According to Ferner (2016), between 2005 and 2011, over 5,500 police officers were arrested (some for multiple types of crimes): over 2,500 police officers were arrested for violence-related crimes, nearly 1,400 police officers were arrested for profit-motivated crimes, nearly 1,300 police officers were arrested for alcohol-related crimes, over 1,000 police officers were arrested for sex-related crimes, and nearly 700 police officers were arrested for drug-related crimes. While around 70% of the arrests resulted in convictions, only around half of the arrests resulted in dismissal.

BREAKDOWNS IN POLICE ACCOUNTABILITY

While every community likely has had to deal with breakdowns in police accountability, large metropolitan areas experience more significant breakdowns in police accountability that reach the attention of the public. The reason for this is simple, larger metropolitan areas have more police officers and more opportunities for police officers to commit criminal behavior without getting caught. We will look at four cases of breakdowns in police accountability from across the United States: The Long Island Cocaine Ring (NY, 1992), the Rampart Scandal (CA, 1998), the Danzinger Bridge Shooting (LA, 2005), and Baltimore GTTF (MD, 2018).

In 1992, five active police officers and one retired police officer were arrested for stealing cocaine from drug dealers in Brooklyn and selling the stolen drugs for a profit in Long Island (New York Post, 2015). In addition to the profits from selling the stolen drugs, the head of Long Island Cocaine Ring, Michael Dowd, ended up earning $8,000 a week (the equivalent of $14,000 a week in 2018) by providing protection to the syndicates. Despite taking no steps to hide his wealth, the NYPD ignored the fact that he was living far beyond the means of a sworn officer, and it was the Suffolk County Police that ended up arresting him. In 2014, they made a movie about the Long Island Cocaine Ring called the Seven Five (Russell, 2014).

The Rampart Scandal involved the corruption of the Community Resources Against Street Hoodlums (CRASH), an anti-gang unit branch of the Rampart Division of the LAPD (Parks, 2000). CRASH gave its members awards for shooting and killing civilians and planted guns on the bodies of civilians shot by CRASH members. In addition, CRASH officers provided protection for gangsters, robbed banks, and stole cocaine from their own evidence room. The city of LA was forced to pay out over $125 million in settlements to settle 140 civil lawsuits resulting from the Rampart Scandal (PBS, 2014).

In the week that followed Hurricane Katrina's devastation of New Orleans, NOPD officers shot and killed two civilians and wounded four more civilians during an incident at the Danziger Bridge (Grimm, 2015). The plain clothes police officers arrived in an unmarked vehicle and did not identify themselves before opening fire on an African American family. When the civilians attempted to flee from the shooters, the plain clothes police officers followed and shot them in the back. Instead of investigating the shooting, the NOPD made up a cover story that falsely stated that the police were responding to an officer down situation, forcing the state and federal government to investigate the shooting (The Times-Picayune, 2011).

The Baltimore PD (BPD) created Baltimore Gun Trace Task Force (GTTF) to deal with guns and violent criminals, but it ended up creating a conspiracy of police misconduct (Fenton, 2018). The Baltimore GTTF ended up providing security for drug dealers, robbing apartments, used toy guns to frame unarmed people that they killed, and conducted illegal searches. The Baltimore's State Attorney General's Office ignored complaints against the GTTF for years before federal authorities took over jurisdiction. Because the Baltimore GTTF targeted suspected criminals within minority communities, they could act with relative impunity for years before they were caught (PBS NewsHour, 2018).

Contrary to the beliefs of some, police accountability exists to protect police officers from civil lawsuits and criminal charges, as well as to protect the local community, so every breakdown in police accountability endangers other police officers as well as harming local communities, whether it involves police officers running drugs or shooting innocent citizens fleeing natural disasters. It protects police officers from lethal retaliation, which seems to be reflected in the data on police fatalities, as the increase in police accountability seems to correspond with a decline in police fatalities, 129 police officer fatalities in 2017 compared to 203 police officer fatalities in 2007 (NLEOCF, 2018). If police officers are held accountable for minor issues early on in their careers by their peers and by their superiors, they will probably be less likely to think that they would be able to get away with major maleficence. It is only by maintaining the public trust that police officers can do their jobs effectively (Frazier, 2007).

THE ROLE OF COMPLEXITY IN POLICE ACCOUNTABILITY

As shown by the previous examples, there are plenty of opportunities for local police officers who are willing to break the law to commit crimes ranging from money laundering to murder with relative impunity until the state and/or federal authorities become aware of their illegal activities. However, few people become police officers with the intention of becoming criminals. Instead, they make one ethical compromise after another, perhaps beginning with looking away when their partner was smacking around a suspect or with demanding cash gratuities from a drug dealer in exchange for not busting them, until they are willing to commit any crime to improve their lives because they believe that their authority will protect them from the consequences of their actions.

What if there was a way for state and/or federal authorities to use complexity to become aware of problematic behavior of local police officers before they reached the point where they were committing crimes? By using methods such as agent-based modeling, state and/or federal authorities should be able to model probable future criminal activity among problematic police officers much as they can model future criminal activity within problematic communities. If they could model probable future criminal activity among problematic police officers, then they could help problematic police officers avoid criminal activity by giving them the counseling and the training that they require to once again become honorable police officers.

The first step in any such program would require a state-wide and/or nation-wide confidential hotline where citizens could make anonymous complaints against local police officers about specific events without fear of reprisal. Based on the frequency of anonymous complaints, the state and/or federal authorities could flag a local police officer for observation and request the personnel file of the local police officer from their superiors. If the personnel file possesses any complaints or reprimands relating to the events of the anonymous complaints, the state and/or federal authorities could request an interview with the local police officer where they would be asked questions to evaluate their personality.

The information from the anonymous complaints, the personnel file, and the interview could then be used to create an agent that could be used to determine contagion risks and criminal risks. In the case of contagion risks, the model would determine the likelihood that the police officer would "infect" other police officers with their behavior. In the case of criminal risks, the model would determine the likelihood that the police officer would escalate their behavior to the point where it would be criminal rather than concerning.

If a local police officer appears to be a high contagion risk, the state and/or federal authorities could offer suggestions to the local police force to minimize possible contagion among between the problematic police officer and other police officers. If the local police force feels that the officer possesses redeeming qualities, they could partner him or her with a more experienced officer to evaluate their behavior and to give them guidance. Alternatively, the local police force could assign the problematic police officer to low status duties where they would have minimal opportunities to abuse their power, like parking violation enforcement, would minimize their standing within the local police force, reducing their credibility and their ability to infect other police officers.

If a local police officer appears to be a high criminal risk though, the state and/or federal authorities could start an official investigation into their activities. If a local police officer is involved in illegal activities, the revelation of such activities can overturn years or decades worth of prosecutions, so it is imperative for society to minimize any potential problems by catching local police officers involved in crimes before it can jeopardize dozens or hundreds of futures cases. If a local police officer is found to have committed crimes, state and/or federal authorities will have to order a review of any cases associated with the corrupt police officer, but justice can only be served if the guilty are punished and the innocent are exonerated.

Conclusion

Within the field of criminal justice policy, we are entering a new era of police accountability as citizens have become empowered by new technologies to demand that they not be abused by police officers. For too long, police officers have been unaccountable for the abuses that they committed against minorities, suspects, and women, but changes in technology now offer a chance for the abused to seek justice against their abusers. Instead of defending the privileges of the social elites, citizens are demanding that police defend the rights of common citizens.

While many police officers serve their communities honorably, it only takes a corrupt minority to turn an entire community against the police force that is supposed to protect them from harm. Whether it is the shooting of a shoplifter, a rape of woman pulled over for a speeding violation, or the harassment of people of color by police officers, the members of communities throughout America have declared through the adoption of video technology that they have had enough of their mistreatment by police officers. Honorable police officers have nothing to fear from public transparency, and it is only corrupt police officers that should fear technology revealing their actions.

In truth, what we are witnessing is a peaceful revolution where technology is preventing the emergence of a violent revolution by allowing abused people to seek justice against people who abuse the authority that they have over them. Peaceful revolutions are preferable to violent revolutions, but violence against authorities will likely be the only alternative left to the abused if society does not deal with corrupt authorities when their actions are revealed through the utilization of technology. It is up to society to society to decide whether it prefers to protect corrupt police officers to violent revolution. In a nation with more firearms than people, violent revolution could be a quite dangerous proposition.

Complexity can be used to help assist in police accountability through allowing state and/or federal authorities to create agent-base models that analyze the risk factors against problematic police officers. By dealing with problematic police officers before they become a problem, or when they are just starting to become corrupted, society will be able to reduce unnecessary trauma to the local community and will be able to increase trust in local police forces by proving to residents that the police are held accountable. While it would likely take years or even decades to completely regain the trust of the local community, every year of progress would result in fewer crimes committed by police officers and would result to more residents coming forward to help police officers with assistance and information.

REFERENCES

Balko, R. (2010, December 7). The war on cameras. *Reason*.

Balko, R. (2014, October 1). U.S. cities pay out millions to settle police lawsuits. *The Washington Post*.

Bayley, D. & Perito, R. (2011). Police corruption: What past scandals teach about current challenges. *United States Institute of Peace*. Retrieved from https://www.usip.org/sites/default/files/SR%20294.pdf

Bedi, M. (2017). The asymmetry of crimes by and against police officers. *Duke Law Journal   Online, 66,* 79–97.

Civil Rights Division (2015). Addressing police misconduct laws enforced by the Department of Justice. *The United States Department of Justice*. Retrieved from https://www.justice.gov/crt/addressing-police-misconduct-laws-enforced-department-justice

Cheney, C. & Robertson, R.V. (2013). Racism and Police Brutality in America. *Journal of African American Studies, 17*(4), 80–508.

COPS (2007). Building trust between the police and the citizens they serve. *U.S. Department of Justice*. Retrieved from http://www.theiacp.org/portals/0/pdfs/buildingtrust.pdf

Department of Justice (2017). Police Reform Finder. Retrieved from https://www.justice.gov/crt/page/file/922456/download

Donovan, K. & Klahm, C. (2015). The role of entertainment media in perception of police use of force. *Criminal Justice and Behavior 42*(12), 1261–1281.

Fenton, J. (2018, February 22). Federal authorities sharing evidence from Baltimore police corruption investigation with local authorities. *The Baltimore Sun*. Retrieved from http://www.baltimoresun.com/news/maryland/crime/bs-md-ci-gttf-evidence-shared-20180221-story.html

Ferner, M. (2016, March 24). Here's how often cops are arrested for breaking the laws they're paid to uphold. *Huffpost*. Retrieved from

https://www.huffingtonpost.com/entry/cops-arrested_us_576c2e13
e4b0cedfa4b9470f

Finn, P. (2001). Citizen review of police: Approaches and implementation. *NCJRS*. Retrieved from https://www.ncjrs.gov/pdffiles1/nij/184430.pdf

Fleetwood, B. (2015, January 15). Police work isn't as dangerous as you may think. *Huffpost*. Retrieved from https://www.huffingtonpost.com/blake-fleetwood/how-dangerous-is-police-w_b_6373798.html

Frazier, S.L. (2007). The loss of public trust in law enforcement. California Commission on Peace Officer Standards and Training. Retrieved from lib.post.ca.gov/lib-documents/cc/40-Frazier.pdf

Gerber, M. (2018, March 12). Monterey Park police officer is convicted of sexually assaulting 3 women during traffic stops. *Los Angeles Times*. Retrieved from http://www.latimes.com/local/lanow/la-me-ln-montery-park-cop-convicted-sexual-assault-20180312-story.html

Grimm, A. (2015, September 4). A decade after Danziger Bridge shooting, killings still cast a shadow. *NOLA*. Retrieved from http://www.nola.com/crime/index.ssf/2015/09/a_decade_after_shootings_danzi.html

Joseph, G. (2016, September 22). From Ferguson to Charlotte, why police protests turn into riots. *Citylab*. Retrieved from https://www.citylab.com/equity/2016/09/from-ferguson-to-charlotte-why-police-protests-turn-into-riots/500981/

Klinger, D.A. (2012). Police training as an instrument of accountability. *Saint Louis University Public Law Review*, 32(1), 111–121.

Krupanski, M. (2012, March 7). Policing the police: Civilian video monitoring of police activity. *The Global Journal*. Retrieved from http://theglobaljournal.net/group/digital-news/article/643/

Muth, K.T. & Jack, N. (2016, September 19). Watching the watchers: Monitoring police performance as public servants. *NLG*. Retrieved from https://www.nlg.org/watching-the-watchers-monitoring-police-performance-as-public-servants/

New York Post (2015, December 28). *5 police corruption scandals that rocked New York City.* Retrieved from https://nypost.com/dispatch/5-police-corruption-scandals-that-rocked-new-york-city/

NLEOCF (2018). *Year-by-year breakdown of law enforcement deaths throughout U.S. history.* Retrieved from http://www.nleomf.org/facts/officer-fatalities-data/year.html

Norwood, C. (2017, May 24). Why California is a case study for monitoring police misconduct. *The Atlantic.* Retrieved from https://www.theatlantic.com/politics/archive/2017/05/police-misconduct-sessions/527664/

Nugent-Borakove, M.E. & Budzilowicz, L.M. (2007). Do lower conviction rates mean prosecutors' offices are performing poorly. American Prosecutors Research Institute. Retrieved from https://www.ndaa.org/pdf/do_lower_conviction_rates_07.pdf

Parks, B.C. (2000, March 1). Board of Inquiry into the Rampart area corruption incident. Los Angeles Police Department. Retrieved from http://assets.lapdonline.org/assets/pdf/boi_pub.pdf

PBS (2014). *The Rampart scandal.* Retrieved from https://www.pbs.org/wgbh/pages/frontline/shows/lapd/scandal/

PBS NewsHour (2018, February 13). How corrupt Baltimore cops used the badge to steal [Video file]. Retrieved from https://www.youtube.com/watch?v=2CvV3DhP5UM

Police Executive Research Forum (2013). Civil rights investigations of local police: Lessons learned. *Critical Issues in Policing Series.* Retrieved from http://www.policeforum.org/assets/docs/Critical_Issues_Series/civil%20rights%20investigations%20of%20local%20police%20-%20lessons%20learned%202013.pdf.

Punyanunt-Carter, N.M. (2008). The perceive realism of African American portrayals on television. *The Howard Journal of Communications, 19,* 241–257.

Quinn, M.W. (2017). How peer intervention training improves policing and community trust. *Minnpost.* Retrieved from https://www.

minnpost.com/community-voices/2017/08/how-peer-intervention-training-improves-policing-and-citizens-trust.

Rose, V. (2013, February 20). Firearm boards in Connecticut and other states. OLR Research Report. Retrieved from https://www.cga.ct.gov/2013/rpt/2013-R-0138.htm

Russell, T. (Director). (2014). *The Seven Five* [Motion Picture]. USA: Sony Pictures.

Schwartz, J.C. (2016). How governments pay: Lawsuits, budgets, and police reform. *UCLA Law Review, 63*, 1144–1298.

The Times-Picayune (2011, July 5). Danzinger Bridge federal trail explained: Time-Picayune video [Video file]. Retrieved from https://www.youtube.com/watch?v=1EExnUJoUx8

UNODC (2011). *Handbook on police accountability, oversight and integrity*. Vienna: United Nations Office.

U.S. Department of Justice (2015). *Why police-community relationships are important. Community Relations Services Toolkit for Policing.* Retrieved from https://www.justice.gov/crs/file/836486/download

Wallace-Wells, B. (2016, July 12). Police shootings, race, and the fear defense. *The New Yorker.* Retrieved from https://www.newyorker.com/news/benjamin-wallace-wells/police-shootings-race-and-the-fear-defense

Zeidman, S. (2005). Policing the police: The role of the courts and the prosecution. *Fordham Urban Law Journal, 32*(2), 99–131.

POLICY
PROCESS

BIPARTISAN POLITICAL GRIDLOCK IN CONGRESS

Mitchell R. Blaszyk

INTRODUCTION

The farewell address of George Washington is often referenced for setting the groundwork of the presidency. Presented September 17th of 1796, Washington spoke in great depths about presidential precedents and government composition. A focal point of Washington's address was the emerging presence of split political parties. The address stated "However [political parties] may now and then answer popular ends, they are likely during time and things, to become potent engines, by which cunning, ambitious, and unprincipled men will be enabled to subvert the power of the people and to usurp for themselves the reins of government, destroying afterwards the very engines which have lifted them to unjust dominion" (Washington, 2008, p. 16). With this statement, Washington expressed his sincere dissenting opinion of rivaling political groups within the United States. Nonetheless, the Federalist and Democratic–Republican parties sprouted deep roots in the American political system; setting the framework for modern-day politics in motion. Since that point in 1796, U.S. politics became accustomed to separate political parties being representative of varying social and ethnic groups with the intention of electing candidates into public office. Over the course of time, discourse between the parties came to be known as "gridlock." Today, Political Gridlock plays a significant role in the functionality of the U.S. political system.

The purpose behind this study was to produce an in-depth analysis of gridlock in Congress and the ethical repercussions which follow this activity. Given the current state of the U.S. political system; this topic stood out as necessary to be studied. As a Political Science major, Political Gridlock, is a familiar topic which plays a predominant role in the innerworkings of government. The reason I chose to study gridlock in Congress was due to the far-reaching consequences it has within society. By breaking this topic down into smaller more tangible pieces; the concept becomes more understandable and the ability to draw conclusions from it becomes closer. My intention with this paper is to highlight the various components constitute Political Gridlock in Congress; and piece them together in a way which displays how politics came to what it is today. Furthermore, I intend to then analyze the indirect and direct ethical consequences which result from Political Gridlock.

The Evolution of the Modern Party System

To understand Political Gridlock, one must first understand the modern evolution of the United States two major political parties. The first pivotal era in time dates to approximately 1936 with the re-election of Democrat, Franklin Roosevelt. Campaigning for the Republican party, Alf Landon opposed the exercise of federal power. Running on the success of his New Deal legislation, Roosevelt was, at the time, one of the first elected Democrats to promote a progressive agenda from what was originally a conservative party. It was after this, that the Democratic party of small government became the Democratic party of large government. As a result, conservatives slowly migrated to the modern-day Republican party. With these political organizations established in their current state, new issues have emerged to contest party success. As much as this oversimplifies the long-rooted history of party politics; this brief overview provides a baseline to refer to. One major dilemma which has plagued Washington and the unity between political officials is that of Bipartisan Political Gridlock. The Oxford Dictionary defines Bipartisanship as quote; "The agreement and cooperation of two political organizations which, in most cases, would oppose each other" (Bipartisan, n.d.). This means that given the proper circumstances emit themselves, political representatives can and will collaborate on legislation across the aisle. One can conclude from this theory, that if prompted to do so, legislators will set aside sentiment from days of old for a greater good. Gridlock can be defined as the instant where these major political organizations fall into stalemate with each other. This means that Conservatives and Liberals are less likely to cooperate on matters of policy and legislation. Because of this, producing these items becomes less likely to reach success in practice.

On a panel discussion in March 2016 at Stanford Law School, with former Congressmen: Mickey Edwards of Oklahoma's 5th district, Dan Lungren of California 3rd district, Barney Frank of Massachusetts 4th district discuss the future of bipartisanship (Persily, 2016). Hosted by the McCoy Family Center for Ethics in Society; there is one segment of the interview which reflects the observed evolution of gridlock in Congress. The former Congressmen, Dan Lungren, remarks in the early part of the discussion of the significance of interaction with his colleagues through family dinners and social events. Describing how while his time in office (2011–2013) as these events became less prevalent over time, so did the level of cooperation between members of opposite parties. This description by the former Congressmen, Lungren, accurately portrays how the decrease in Social Capitol over time played a direct role in the amount of unity felt between elected officials. As seen through the series of events described, modern history has established an unsustainable means of producing policy.

THE IMPACT OF POLITICAL GRIDLOCK

Currently, the issue remains, that Political Gridlock in Congress threatens to continue to engulf representatives in an unsustainable state of conflict. One example of this strife is using "slang" terms meant to depict weak party members as disaffected. The terms: R.I.N.O. and D.I.N.O. are both used in the context that representatives of the respective party side with those other than their corresponding party. Republican and Democrat in Name Only (R.I.N.O. and D.I.N.O., respectively) portray a significant level of dissatisfaction by party members toward those whom are willing to cross the isle and collaborate with members outside of their political organization. That is, by siding with others whom are not of the same party on political matters, said party officials will be ousted and characterized as disloyal. This illustration is momentous, as it amplifies the effect to which representatives will refuse to come together (Ormont, 2016, p. 1)

Another such example of this cut-throat relationship between institutions is the application of litmus tests. The Washington Post describes political litmus tests as individual ethical or policy-based concerns which are then used to place persons along party lines (Kliff, 2011). One such case is the ethical controversy of abortion. This procedure is the one which often acts as an aria of conflict along both party lines. Incoming politicians are often questioned on this topic and their stance while campaigning; resulting in a scenario where one topic will make or break whether a candidate receives party backing. This example portrays a practice where siding adversely on an issue will result in legisla-tors being excommunicated from the graces of the party. Such an action fortifies the notion that cooperation between parties is both stratified and limited. In an extended study published in 2017 by Pew Research Center (Mitchell, 2017); it was found that partisan division in the Unit-ed States among the general population has escalated dramatically.

Given the decrease in cooperation between Congressional Democrats and Republicans, there are a variety of ethical repercussions which have resulted from this circumstance. One such example is that of govern-ment productivity. Notre Dame Journal of Law, Ethics & Public Policy stated, "In 2011, citing gridlock in Congress, Standard & Poor's down-graded the United States' debt rating to AA+ for the first time in history" (Catanese, 2014, p. 324). This study shows how the negative exchange between party representatives has a direct effect on productivity off Congress. Effects of the debt and the stalemate in congress which sur-rounds it have a direct effect on average citizens. In an article produced by Reuters, analyzing a study from the Harvard School of Business found quote: "A majority of the school's alumni surveyed said they be-lieved the US political system was hurting the economy (Malone, 2016, p. 16)." The surveys included responses from 4,807 alumni of Harvard Business School from May 3rd through June 6th and 1,048 members of the public polled June 10th–26th. The public survey had a margin of error of 3.3 percentage points, margin of error does not apply to the alumni survey as it was not a random sample survey (Malone, 2016, p. 16). Re-uters highlights in this article the significance of third-party effects of political disputes. By decreasing productivity in D.C., members of the public at large are affected in a negative way. Another political tool which is employed which strengthens this divide is the development of gerry-mandered districts. Encyclopedia Britannica defines Gerrymandering as; "drawing the boundaries of electoral districts in a way that gives one party an unfair advantage over its rivals" (Gerrymandering, n.d.). This process of creating safe seats for Congressmen ensures they will remain loyal to party lines. Given officials are in protected districts where they run unopposed; if they prove to go outside party lines, another member of the same party can run and will win. It is for this reason that gerry-mandered districts are responsible for promoting bipartisan gridlock.

CONCLUSION

With escalating tensions between political entities within the United States reaching a peak; one must question the ethical and political repercussions which will certainly continue to follow. Through the evolution of American politics, various levels of discourse have been found to be present. Living in the modern era, the challenges, which are faced by Washington as significant as they may be, are never without solutions. During Abraham Lincoln's 1838 address before the Young Men's Lyceum of Springfield; Lincoln describes how resilient the United States is to outside forces, yet vulnerable from within. Lincoln says; "Shall we expect some transatlantic military giant to step the ocean and crush us at a blow? Never! All the armies of Europe, Asia, and Africa combined, with all the treasure of the earth (our own excepted) in their military chest, with a Bonaparte for a commander, could not by force take a drink from the Ohio or make a track on the Blue Ridge in a trial of a thousand years. At what point then is the approach of danger to be expected? I answer. If it ever reaches us it must spring up amongst us; it cannot come from abroad. If destruction be our lot we must ourselves be its author and finisher" (Lincoln, 1984, p. 2). This sentiment serves as a starch reminder to the responsibilities of American people. Through moments of conflict and animosity, Americans must rally together for common good. Although the United States hosts a wide variety of ideologies; at the center of them all is a passion for this nation. Gridlock, which divides the country, will serve as an issue which Americans must come together to solve.

REFERENCES

Bipartisan (n.d.). In Oxford Dictionaries Online. Retrieved from https://en.oxforddictionaries.com/definition/bipartisan

Catanese, N.S. (2014). Gerrymandered gridlock: addressing the hazardous impact of partisan redistricting. *Notre Dame Journal of Law, Ethics & Public Policy, 28*(1), 323–351.

Gerrymandering (n.d.). In Encyclopedia Britannica Online. Retrieved from www.britannica.com/topic/gerrymandering.

Kliff, S. (2011, October 24). How abortion became a political litmus test. *The Washington Post.* Retrieved from www.washingtonpost.com/blogs/ezra-klein/post/how-abortion-became-a-political-litmus-test/2011

Lincoln, A. (1984). The perpetuation of our political institutions (Address by Abraham Lincoln before the Young Men's Lyceum of Springfield, January 27, 1838). *Journal of the Abraham Lincoln Association,* 6(1), 6–14.

Malone, S. (2016, September 14). Americans blame Washington gridlock for slow economic growth: Study. *Reuters.* Retrieved from https://www.reuters.com/article/us-usa-politics-economy-survey/americans-blame-washington-gridlock-for-slow-economic-growth-study-idUSKCN11L06Z

Mitchell, T. (2017). Political polarization, 1994–2017. *Pew Research Center for the People and the Press.* Retrieved from www.people-press.org/interactives/political-polarization-1994-2017/.

Ormont, M. (2016, May 22). RINO's and DINO's. *Daily Kos.* Retrieved from www.dailykos.com/stories/2016/5/22/1529350/-RINO-s-and-DINO-s.

Persily, Nate (2016, March 23). Gridlock: Is there a future for bipartisanship? Stanford Law School. Retrieved from www.youtube.com/watch?v=mmNfsz5laJc.

Washington, G. (2008). Washington's farewell address (1796). *Avalon Project.* Retrieved from http://avalon.law.yale.edu/18th_century/washing.asp

SECURITY
POLICY

THE ENEMY OF CYBER SPACE

Chad Wilson

INTRODUCTION

Tampa Florida, an 11-year-old male gained access to his middle school computer system to change his grades (Masnick, 2003). This young male was arrested, released, and forced to attend a diversion course where he learned the "wrongs" of his action/s. I want to draw your attention to three things the boy's age of 11 years old, his actions of infiltrating a computer system beyond his perceived intellect, and finally his punishment of legal detainment and required completion of a diversion course. This is only one of many cases that have taken place across the nation with similar outcomes and in some cases, the outcomes are far worse. Should we really punish the youth for discovering and using the skills we need and will need in the future? Is it fair to nudge our youth into programming only to punish those who find the flaws in professionals' code?

Current research shows that many Americans are worried about hackers and what they may do to/with their information (McCarthy, 2017). This assumes of course that all hackers are cyber criminals and have malicious intent toward most if not all systems they encounter. Throughout this document, I analyze the above questions and assumptions from the viewpoint of a student in pursuit of a B.S in Computer Science with a focus on Cyber Security and a minor in Psychology and an intern at a Network Solutions company.

WHO IS A HACKER?

The current definition of a hacker is misused in popular media/social interactions to mean a cybercriminal of sorts (i.e. hacktivist, cyber terrorist, cyber drug dealer, etc.). According to Gregory T. Donovan and Cindi Katz in their article "Cookie Monsters: Seeing Young People's Hacking as Creative Practice," they state that "in the post-9/11 security state *hacking* is understood as cybercrime—politically motivated or otherwise—that is a threat to national security, corporate security, and personal safety" (Donovan & Katz, 2009, p. 205). They go further as to explain how a hacker was originally perceived as "commonly defined in relation to computer/network security, the free and open-source soft-ware (FOSS) movement, and/or general computer hobbyists." This is the working definition for this paper and the one I will refer to through-out my writing. In modern American society, we rely heavily on our technological infrastructures; as such, we need to prepare a new kind of warrior to serve and protect our online interests/properties and the information that is coupled with them. According to Raja (2014), com-puter science is the least taken course in high schools across the nation.

This tags along with Microsoft, Facebook, Twitter, Apple, and many oth-er tech giants call for the education system to begin teaching computer coding as an essential skill to children throughout their K-12 careers. The shortage of youth that can code is concerning when we look at the number of youth punished for using code the "wrong" way. The "wrong" way of course being the use of coding skills to shed light on and exploit flaws in current programs and systems alike. Emmanuel Goldstein, edi-tor of 2,600, has described this situation in the following way: "Hackers have become scapegoats: We discover the gaping holes in the system and then get blamed for the flaws" (Gunkel, 2000). Gunkel (2000) goes on to elaborate Goldstein's statements by asserting that hackers are drawn to the computer as a challenge to solve a puzzle. This draw is a compul-sion brought on by the flaws in the design of the system itself.

WHY EVERYONE SHOULD BE A HACKER

I argue that the methodology of hacking must be taught to youth who show an interest in learning how to become a hacker. Teaching the youth to hack like the criminals they will face when working in the cy-ber security sector will better prepare them to fight on the front lines of cyberspace. The ethical dilemma that humans have faced in history over creating child warriors who will learn to become the fiercest and most cunning of fighters is far different in cyberspace. Unlike a physical battlefield where the objective is barbaric in nature and holds extreme consequences (i.e. death), cyber space is a battle of the minds where the consequences are only dealt to those found guilty of (societally per-ceived) unethical actions.

We must begin exposing the youth to hacking at a young age. This allows the youth who will end up in various fields such as Systems Engineering, Software Development, IT Management, etc. to gain exposure with their respective areas and how these areas can and often will be infiltrated and/or exploited. The same exposure allows future cyber security professionals to possess not only the knowledge that their enemies will use, it also allows for the creative edge that we gain from childhood "play" to fuel the conceptualization of future attack vectors and implement the proper mitigation tactics necessary to suppress and eliminate the threat. Without these abilities, professionals will be unable to protect their companies from cyber-attacks (Radziwill, 2015).

There is opposition to the idea of teaching cyber-security through the method of thinking like a hacker to catch a hacker. Several malware companies have stated they will not hire students being taught by a University to create malware and learn the ways of a criminal (Kushner, 2010). The idea that teaching 20 people how to hack and having one out of the 20 become a criminal with their new-found knowledge is a risk some are not willing to take. When the topic of "white-hat/grey-hat" hackers arises into argument, the point becomes that although they may begin with no mal-intent "since they were rarely caught and disciplined, they formed the moral value that if they do no harm to others, it is not wrong to benefit themselves" (Xu, Hu, & Zhang, 2013, p. 73). This would mean that a self-proclaimed "ethical" hacker could also be crossing a line between societies ethical standards and the standards of the hacker. Teaching the youth how to hack without consequence (getting caught) to understand how to defend against malicious agents in cyber space may inadvertently lead them to walk the fine line between what is ethical and unethical (Radziwill, Romano, Shorter, & Benton, 2015).

SECURITY AND PREPARATION

The themes of this paper play in two predominate fields: the first being Security and the second being Preparation through education. Security is the overall theme to understanding the dilemmas facing society regarding cyberspace. Preparation through education is the theme regarding the way we implement security into a working environment. Teaching the youth how to hack will better prepare the future workforce to deal with and eliminate threats poised against their respective fields.

I argue that the theme of security is the most important when thinking about issues in cyber space modern society is currently facing because, without security, there is no conceivable way to stop malevolent agents from disrupting and/or destroying infrastructures full of valuable data. People in our current society must understand that no system is 100 percent secure and should be mindful of how much data they store and in what locations, their data is being stored. The first step in security starts at the individual level. If complacency clouds an individual's judgment over their level of security, then proper measures should be in place to fall back on. This should not discount the importance of preparation through education because security is the fruit that stems from the labor put forth by rigorous hours of education and preparation. Society must keep in mind the fact that without learning from experience, an individual is not truly prepared. Experience being subjective in the sense that a person may gather experience from emotional stimuli derived from reading about a method or event or the person may gather it through the means of physically altering and manipulating an object.

Conclusion

Thus, we arrive to a conclusion that the path toward a secure cyber space begins with the focus on the youth, education, and security. Though many may argue that it is a risk to teach the youth how to hack due an infinite amount of possibilities regarding their own ethical standards and the fact that there are many people who will cross the ethical boundaries, the amount of people who will remain in the field of ethical play will counter if not triumph over the former. The key is to develop an ethical group of hackers large enough and young enough to remain updated on new and upcoming trends in cyber security. This is conceived from the argument many have about educating the youth to perform acts of defiance toward the way a system designed to be accessed to find a "hole" that can be exploited.

This conclusion is significant because it is an idea that cannot produce immediate results. The fact that results are not immediate is often grounds for dismissal in our "right now" world. However, I assert that there is beauty in work that flourishes over time impacting generations to come rather than the generation here and now. Allowing these ideas to evolve over time will show the true power of human ingenuity and what can be accomplished when we remember to plan for the inevitable first and the possible second. Plans that will not reach fruition for quite some time are tricky and require the utmost attention to detail when running through all possible scenarios. This conclusion calls for a plan that has two stages the first is educating individuals how to find and identify threats and then implement the long-term goals and mitigation solutions they have discovered through years of research and practical application.

References

Donovan, G.T. & Katz, C. (2009). Cookie Monsters: Seeing young people's hacking as creative practice. *Children, Youth and Environments, 19* (1), 197–222.

Gunkel, D.J. (2000). Hacking cyberspace: An introduction. *JAC: A Journal of Composition Theory, 20*(4), 797–823.

Kushner, A.B. (2010, March 13). College teacher shows students how to be hackers. *Newsweek.*

Retrieved December 12, 2017, from http://www.newsweek.com/college-teacher-shows-students-how-be-hackers-87657

Masnick, M. (2003, February 12). 11-year old arrested for changing his grades. *(Mis)Uses of Technology.* Podcast retrieved from https://www.techdirt.com/articles/20030212/1245223.shtml

McCarthy, N. (2017, November 8). The crimes Americans worry about most. Statista. Retrieved from https://www.statista.com/chart/11735/the-crimes-americans-worry-about-most/

Radziwill, N., Romano, J., Shorter, D., & Benton, M. (2015). The ethics of hacking: Should it be taught? *Cornell University Library.* Retrieved from https://www.researchgate.net/publication/286513391_The_Ethics_of_Hacking_Should_It_Be_Taught

Radziwill, Y. (2015). *Cyber-attacks and the exploitable imperfection of international law.* Boston, MA: Brill Nijhoff.

Raja, T. (2014, June 16). Is coding the new literary: Why America's schools need to train a generation of hackers. *Mother Jones.* Retrieved from https://www.motherjones.com/media/2014/06/computer-science-programming-code-diversity-sexism-education/

Xu, Z., Hu, Q., & Zhang, C. (2013). Why computer talents become computer hackers. *Communications of the ACM, 56*(4), 64–74.

SOCIAL
POLICY

THE ETHICS AND GLOBAL IMPACT OF JIU-JITSU

Ryan L. Russell.

INTRODUCTION

When is conflict ethical? What actions are justified during a conflict? What suffering, what pain, what horror can a human being inflict upon another human being before it stops being self-defense and just becomes brutality?

If we peel back the layers of history to observe a situation such as the Holocaust, it is distinguishable as an act that was brutal, inhumane, and abhorrent for obvious reasons. Yet if we transition earlier, to a period in history such as the Battle of Thermopylae or more widely known as the Battle of 300; not only is combat deemed necessary but it is also looked upon as just and heroic. The purpose of this writing is to detail a specific style of combat relevant to today—"Jiu-Jitsu." This writing serves to answer three main questions related to the topic—Is Jiu-Jitsu an ethical practice? In what ways is it so? And what is its application. We may begin deconstructing and synthesizing this ethical dilemma by identifying and summarizing terms.

1. Ethical: "The proper role of ethical reasoning is to highlight acts of two kinds: those which enhance the well-being of others ... and those that harm or diminish the well-being of other ..." (Paul & Elder, p. 3, 2013).

2. Brazilian Jiu-Jitsu/ BJJ: An act of weaponless fighting employing chokes, joint locks, and throws to subdue or disable an opponent (GracieMag, 2007).

3. Mixed Marital Arts/ MMA: A full contact combat sport that encompasses a wide variety to fighting styles and techniques to include striking, kicking, grappling, and submissions (Singpatong Sitnumnoi, 2013).

General assumptions related to this topic include the sport being considered a barbaric practice and inhumane. Owing to the perceived barbarism, it is then postulated that all practitioners are violent by nature and thus, there is no inherent skill possessed by practitioners. And lastly, the practice may not be perceived as distinguished as some other sports (Boxing, Judo, Wrestling, and Tae Kwon Do). My view on the matter is not only that of a college student, but of a practitioner to the art of Jiu-Jitsu.

Purpose

This writing serves to identify the Ethics of Jiu-Jitsu as well as its global impact. Questions addressed specifically by this writing are; Is Jiu-Jitsu an Ethical practice? In what ways is this practice Ethical? How does this apply to people? And lastly how does this apply to MMA? Anecdotal evidence collected and used in this writing was taken from a sample of individuals across multiple physiological backgrounds. This evidence was then compared against individuals who practice in at least one form of traditional martial arts as well as against individuals who did not participate in any form of physical activities (Vertonghen & Theeboom, 2010). Findings within the research suggest that nonpractitioners and nontraditional practitioners generally show less positive emotions (Vertonghen & Theeboom, 2010). Congruently, research gathered suggested that female traditional practitioners were more likely to respond aggressively in hostile confrontation rather than their male counterparts (Vertonghen & Theeboom, 2010). From the research, I argue that within the realm of martial arts, Jiu-jitsu is an ethical practice with rules and standards in place to ensure the well-being of participants. Also, based primarily off the virtues upon which the sport was conceived, it has in place themes that convey a sense of self-awareness and sportsmanship that suggest there is more to the practice than combat alone. In relation to the individual, there seems to be a distinct and favorable impact upon those who are actively participating in the practice, which services a greater utilitarian effort of fostering a peaceful environment for people.

Background

To provide background in a geographical context to Jiu-Jitsu, the following shall serve as a summarization of its impact and less as a detailed account. Originating in Japan as a derivative of Judo, Jiu-Jitsu began with one founder in the late 1800s; Matsuyo Maeda (Skidmore, 1991). Maeda subsequently brought the practice to Brazil and passed his knowledge on to friends Luis Franca and Carlos Gracie (Skidmore, 1991). As the knowledge base grew and diversified throughout the generations of the Gracie family, it was here that the practice took on the prefix "Brazilian" giving Jiu-Jitsu solidarity and identity in its new-found home. The practice later spread to Israel, Germany, and America and began a new phenomenon in its wake; mixed martial arts or "MMA."

The following are facts deemed relevant in substantiating the claim of Jiu-Jitsu's ethicality.

- The fundamental ideas of Martial Arts descend from Zen Buddhism in China (Skidmore, p. 131, 1991).

- Jiu-Jitsu was originally derived from Judo in Japan (Green & Svinth, 2010).

- BJJ is the world's second most popular Martial Art (Singpatong Sitnumnoi, 2013).

- Practitioners of traditional martial arts emphasize more humility, self-confidence, and negative energy control than nontraditional practitioners/competitors (Vertonghen & Theeboom, 2010).

These facts give us information sufficient enough to draw inferences from in the discussion of who may be harmed and benefitted by this practice. There are essentially two groups of people who may be harmed, the first of such are practitioners of Jiu-jitsu due to sport-related injuries or physical altercations. The second group of people who have potential to be harmed are the individuals who get into the physical altercations with practitioners. As we advance, we move to the groups of people who stand to benefit from BJJ's practice and there are three. The first of these groups are the individuals and the organizations that provide instruction. Aside from capital gain, their group stands to gain doubly because they have a commodity that people want and by providing it, they in turn increases their visibility and market value. The second group of people who stand to gain are the practitioners due to the physical and psychological effects experienced because of training. And lastly, the third group that stands to gain is the public. The public is understood to benefit indirectly by way of the practitioners, which is implied by the overall composed nature of the practitioners and is placed into effect upon interaction.

Ethics

In pursuit of determining the ethicality of BJJ, I have identified themes and concepts relevant to such. The first two concepts highlight the ethics of the practice and speak to the core of its existence and proliferation.

1. Relating to people in ethically appropriate ways; Polite, Courteous, Respectful, Tactful (Paul & Elder, 2013).

2. Acting out of concern to behave ethically; Scrupulous, Honorable, And Upright (Paul & Elder, 2013). That is—Bettering one's self.

I have conversely identified two concepts that speak to any perceived unethical behaviors in the practice of BJJ.

1. Using Intellectual skills to get others to Act Against their own Best Interest; Cunning, Trickery (Paul & Elder, 2013). That is—Manipulation of movement and force.

2. Causing Pain or Suffering; Dominate, Hurt (Paul & Elder, 2013). That is—Intentional control of an opponent with pain.

Themes

In the act of processing facts such as historical and geographical information about Jiu-Jitsu, we were able to make distinctions about its ethics. Moving forward, I discerned underlying themes relevant to its ethics. The four themes selected are Honor, Discipline, Self-Awareness, and Sportsmanship. I argue that Honor is the most important theme because honor is a fundamental piece of the warrior ethos. It is also in some cultures and belief systems considered honorable to be polite, courteous, respectful, and the likes. I contend that discipline is the second most important theme because it is understood that to better the self, one must be committed, and to be committed is to be disciplined. I assert that self-awareness is the third most important theme, and this is because without self-awareness, one is unable to know if there exists a need to better the self in the mental or the spiritual. The last theme I have elected as important is sportsmanship. This theme is important because it encompasses all the ideals that I have covered thus far and is the foundation of the interaction specific to competitive sports.

Regarding the information presented previously, we may rightly conclude the following. Martial arts involve fighting techniques, mental discipline, physical exercise, and various philosophical and intellectual concepts. These concepts include among others, the virtue of balance from the doctrine of Taoism, and the virtue of breathing from the doctrine of Buddhism. Martial arts practitioners may necessarily be perceived as having more positive emotions than nonpractitioners. And lastly, BJJ is the world's second most popular martial art however, may be regarded as more ethical due to its concepts and execution.

In closing, as we draw parallels between the application of such understandings to the individual, it may be stated that there are varying positive effects from participation in the practice of BJJ. These effects include but are not limited to problem-solving, emotion management, and of course increased sociability. These skills are important because they allow an individual to obtain clarity in developing thought and to effectively communicate in the real world. As is relates to combat, it may be stated that Jiu-Jitsu is an ethical practice-based simply off its core values. These values are restraint, graciousness, and compassion. These values are important to modern combat because they add integrity to a form of combat that can be considered devoid of the original substance from which it was originally conceived. Accordingly, there are links to the rise of Mixed Martial Arts competition and the expansion of Jiu-Jitsu. These ties allow us to acknowledge Jiu-Jitsu as an integral part of the diverse world of Combat Sports and the development of Mixed Martial Arts as a sport.

REFERENCES

GracieMag (2007). The history of Jiu-Jitsu. Retrieved from http://www.graciemag.com/en/the-saga-of-jiu-jitsu/

Green, T.A. & Svinth, J.R. (2010). Martial arts of the world: An encyclopedia of history and innovation. Santa Barbara, CA: ABC-CLIO.

Paul, R. & Elder, L (2013). The thinkers guide to understanding the foundations of ethical reasoning: Based on critical thinking concepts

& tools. *Foundation for Critical Thinking.* Retrieved from https://www. criticalthinking.org/store/get_file.php?inventories_id=169

Singpatong Sitnumnoi (2013). Start your Muay Thai Career with us. Retrieved from www.singpatong-sitnumnoi.com/

Skidmore, M.J. (1991). Oriental contributions to western popular culture: The martial arts. *Journal of Popular Culture, 25*(1), 129–148.

Vertonghen, J. & Theeboom, M. (2010). The social-psychological outcomes of martial arts practise among youth: A review. *Journal of Sports Science and Medicine 9,* 528–537.

TECHNOLOGY
POLICY

THE SMART HOME WILL INCREASE BENEFIT FOR HUMAN LIFE

Khai Lim

INTRODUCTION

For many years, Home Automation is mainly used as a feature of science fiction writing, but it's become practical since the early of the twentieth century that is because of the introduction of electricity and rapid improvement in information technology. Home automation or smart homes is described as a technology which is used within the home environment to provide comfort, security, convenience, and energy efficiency to its user or occupants. By inclusion of the Internet of Things (IoTs), the research and development of home automation are going to become more and more popular. Different wireless technologies that support remote data transfer, control and sensing such as RFID, Wi-Fi, Bluetooth, and cellular networks have been evolved to add intelligence at various levels in the home (Jain & Vijaygopalan, 2010). In the base of the smart home problems, I will try answer critical thinking question to analyze who is smart home? What are the opportunities available? what is good and what can be changed? A smart home or building is a home or building that is equipped with special structured wiring to enable occupants to remotely control or program an array of automated home electronic devices by entering a single command. For example, a homeowner on vacation can use a Touchtone phone to arm a home security system, control temperature gauges, switch appliances on or off, control lighting, program a home theater or entertainment system, and perform many other tasks. On my point of view as a student in neutral, we are living in technology century that how make the life is more easier and how technology support and help people have more convenience. Homeowner may control and protect their property with camera security provide. Cyber risk management strategies must also include vigilance to know when an attack happens and resilience after a breach.

THE IoT INDUSTRY

The IoT industry is going to be a very fast-growing market. According to the article from Phys.org, it is projected to become a 7.1 trillion market in 2020 (Spencer, 2014). With that much growth, it is not a shock to see the two biggest names in the mobiles device industry, Apple and Google battling for market share. When looking at how Google is taking on the IoT marketplace, you can look to how they are using their market share in the mobile device operating system to expand their offerings. The purpose this article will show what does the benefit of home automation bring for homeowner. The home automation is automating the ability to control items around the house from window shades to pet feeders with a simple push of a button or a voice command. Some activities, like setting up a lamp to turn on and off at your whim, are simple and relatively inexpensive. Other, like advanced surveillance cameras, may require a more serious investment of time and money. There are many smart home product categories, so homeowner can control everything from lights and temperature to locks and security in your home. In fact, Keen home is a group focuses on improving the systems that keep a home running and maintain them (Lee, 2017). By embedding short-range mobile transceivers into a wide array of additional gadgets and every item, enabling new forms of communication between people and things, and between things themselves (ITU, 2005). IoT can expand Kenya's economy by 250% by 2025 (Riaga, 2015). Several Stellar smart home devises have already hit the market and made their way into thousands of houses around the world. The IoT creates a lot of profit to security company and who made the apps help control the house simpler. The homeowner is also inherence the profit that they can control, command, keep check, and maintain their home easier. The harm from the IoT could be family finance, not help for old generation to keep follow the technology, the homeowner may have lost the data.

I argue the safety policy in smart home is the most important theme because it was a first thing homeowner and consumer want to understand clearly what smart homes create a benefit for them. I argue that utilitarian theme is also important because consumer always look at the benefit technology bring for them and think about it before giving decision to buy them, or when the company like Google, Apple; they will look at the how much it will be sharing to create their own benefit.

CONCLUSION

This paper I discussed how the IoT is going to change and create the interest personal and benefit for social life with the way smart home is viewed in the future. With the additional technologies that are present and being developed to control the home, two major rivals are battling for market share in what is being projected to become a $7.1 trillion-dollar market. In this paper, I discussed the privacy concerns that the IoT can become and how they are being used in the company's current business models. I also discussed how these technologies operate and what protocols they will use to transmit this information to the user. The way to look at Internet gave us was the opportunity to connect in way we could never have dreamed possible. The IoTs will take us beyond connection to become a part of a living moving global nervous system. Whether you are an individual, technology developer or adopter of these technologies, the IoT will stretch the boundaries of today's system. The conclusion is very significant because it gave us to see a big map of see farther in future and emphasize the IoT will change our life.

REFERENCES

ITU (2005). *ITU Internet reports 2005: The Internet of things*. Retrieved from http://www.itu.int/osg/spu/publications/internetofthings/ InternetofThings_summary.pdf

Jain, P.C. & Vijaygopalan, K.P. (2010). RFID and wireless sensor networks. *Proceedings of ASCNT, 5*, 1–11.

Lee, E. (2017, October 11). IoT will create the future we've been waiting for. Retrieved from https://keenhome.io/blogs/community/iot-will-create-the-future-weve-been-waiting-for

Riaga, O. (2015). IoT can expand Kenya's economy by 250% by 2025. *Kenya Tech News*. Retrieved from https://www.kachwanya.com/2015/04/30/iot/

Spencer, L. (2014, June 5). Internet of Things market to hit $7.1 trillion by 2020: IDC. *ZDNet*. Retrieved from https://www.zdnet.com/article/internet-of-things-market-to-hit-7-1-trillion-by-2020-idc/

QUANTUM COMPUTING: APPLICATIONS AND IMPLICATIONS TO CRYPTOLOGY

Peter Lambert

INTRODUCTION

There are lots of new technologies that are in development. Computer scientists have a responsibility to understand these new technologies and their impacts on society. Perhaps, one of the least widely understood emerging technology is quantum computing. A major difference between conventional and quantum computing is that a quantum computer uses quantum bits, more commonly known as qubits, rather than binary digits. A qubit could be anything that has two quantum states. An electron could be a qubit, and the two quantum states could be whether it is spinning up or down. The physical difference between a qubit and a conventional bit is that a qubit can exist in a linear combination of its two states. This means a qubit has a probability of being in one state or the other when observed. A quantum computers strength comes from using this and other quantum phenomena, such as quantum entanglement.

EXPLAINING QUANTUM COMPUTING

But how are conventional computers and quantum computers functionally different? A quantum computer can run any classical algorithm (Lanzagorta & Uhlmann, 2009). This does not mean it can run the same algorithm faster. The bulk of classical algorithms are not sped up when ran on a quantum computer (Ozhigov, 1999). That is why a quantum computers strength comes from the special algorithms made for them. These special algorithms are called quantum algorithms. A quantum algorithm is any algorithm that takes advantage of the physically unique traits of quantum mechanics. Access to these quantum algorithms is what gives quantum computers their impressively fast operating times for certain problems.

One quantum algorithm that is impressively fast compared to a conventional algorithm is Grover's algorithm for searching an entry in a nonordered dataset (Strubell, 2011). The conventional algorithm would have to search each entry of a dataset to find the correct one. Grover's algorithm can find the correct entry in only a square root of the operations required in a conventional computer. This means the larger the dataset, the more efficient Grover's algorithm becomes. For a dataset of 100 entries, Grover's algorithm can find the correct entry 10 times faster. For a dataset of one million entries, Grover's algorithm can find the solution in a thousandth of the operations!

While powerful, these quantum algorithms are not enough to make a conventional computer obsolete. Most people seem to be under the impression that quantum computers will completely replace conventional computers. For most of what a standard consumer needs, a quantum computer will not speed it up. Researchers have not yet come up with a quantum algorithm for streaming videos of cats yet. That doesn't change how much the subject has been hyped up to the general population.

THE CAPABILITIES OF QUANTUM COMPUTING

When people talk about quantum computing, they claim it will revolutionize mankind. In the same way that fire, or the wheel did. Quantum computing when combined with machine learning could affect every aspect of human life (Waddell, 2017). Machine learning is a program that has application in many fields. It has seen use in cancer research (Waddell, 2017). Quantum machine learning is an emerging technology that tries to merge quantum physics and machine learning (Schuld, Sinayskiy, & Petruccione, 2014). With the development of stronger quantum computers, these machine learning algorithms can become faster. Machine learning is not the only major application for quantum computing. Because of certain quantum algorithms, there are lots of implications for cryptology. The current algorithms we are using for encryption are easily solved on a quantum computer running Shor's algorithm (Shor, 1995). This compounded with how underdeveloped our critical infrastructures cybersecurity is, could prove to be a real national security threat once quantum computers are cheap and commercially available. Current quantum computers also aren't quite yet powerful enough to solve any modern widely used cryptography algorithms (Gershon, 2013). There are communities that are working on developing quantum proof encryption. These encryption methods can withstand an attack from a quantum computer.

Once quantum computers are widely available cheap, and powerful, then old cybersecurity systems will become obsolete very quickly. Any business or private network could be broken into quite easily using a quantum computer. This could mean a complete overhaul for security as we know it. If a hacker had access to a powerful quantum computer, then every companies' encryption algorithms would be broken easily.

The international intelligence communities have a vested interest in staying at the head of quantum encryption. Russia is already suspected of hacking into power plants in the United States (Perlroth & Sanger, 2018). These attacks put the Russian hackers in control of several critical facilities. They were capable of locking people out of their systems and supplied clear evidence of the ability to control and shutdown power plants.

It is believed Russian hackers have already pulled the plug on power plants before. In December 2015, hackers turned off the power for 230,000 Ukrainian citizens. The Ukrainian government reports the Russians were responsible (Sanger, 2016). This was the first known international cyberattack on a power grid. American business owners should be alarmed at this knowledge. Any business related to critical infrastructure would be the first targets for a cyberattack.

The past few years have made it obvious that critical infrastructure is now a major target for attacks from hackers and governments (Derene, 2009). These attacks have the potential for massive damage. It would be possible for an international cyberattack to affect water, power, data centers, defense systems, and just about anything connected to the Internet. The current security for these systems have been proved to be not sufficient for any serious attack, and hackers have proved their ability to take control of our most critical systems. It is going to be every nations priority to be able to defend against serious cyber-attacks.

The cyber-attacks of the future are going to be performed on quantum computers. Once a quantum computer is made that is capable of breaking modern popular cryptographic algorithms, then anyone with a nonquantum proof algorithm would be broken into in a comparatively trivial amount of time. The NSA in August 2016 released a document that warned data-oriented businesses about the threat of quantum computing (Simonite, 2016). In the past, the NSA has informed businesses what kinds of algorithms should be safe from attack, but this document details how the threat of quantum computing compromises the currently used algorithms.

The U.S. government has been researching and developing quantum computers. The Army research office has been the government body that has headed development in quantum computing. The U.S. government spends $250 million a year on quantum computer research (Cho, 2018). Just recently, the Department of Energy has started a $40 million venture to help develop quantum computers.

Quantum computers could solve modern encryption algorithms easily because of their ability to process Shor's algorithm. The modern encryption methods we use today count on how difficult it is to solve three math problems. The integer factorization problem, elliptic-curve discrete logarithm problem, and the discrete logarithm problem are the difficult math problems currently used in popular cryptographic algorithms.

At their root, these three problems are factoring problems. A factoring problem is finding the smallest whole numbers that multiply into the number you are interested in. There is no known mathematical definition for a hard problem. However, these problems could be considered hard because there are no known algorithms that solve these problems in polynomial time, and progress has been slow in developing an algorithm that solves these functions quickly. Unfortunately, there is no guarantee that these algorithms cannot be solved in any reasonable time, and there will always be people making advances in computational power and more efficient mathematical algorithms. The longest number to be factored was an RSA number of bit length 768 (Kleinjung et al., 2010). It was done using about 2,000 years of computational power over the course of two years. These encryptions are so difficult to break, that whoever can factor one of these numbers is rewarded with money. The highest amount of cash rewarded was for RSA-768 for $50,000. An online commercial encryption typically has an RSA key with a length of 1024 bit. Factoring a 1024-bit RSA modulus is about 1,000 times harder than factoring a 768-bit one (Kleinjung et al., 2010). Despite this, it is obvious that it is becoming more and more possible to do something that must be impossible for the sake of security. Using current non-quantum algorithms, the day isn't so far off that the standard for encryption will be simple to break.

The way a conventional computer finds prime factorizations is through brute forcing a solution. The biggest advances in improving this have gone into more intelligently selecting numbers for testing a solution. The best algorithm for this is a number field sieve.

Along with this conventional algorithm, there has been a surge in the past few years in GPU programming. GPU programming uses the huge number of processors on a GPU, and having each processor run the same algorithm on different parts of information. This concept is known as parallelism. A GPU can run an otherwise extremely intensive chunk of code quite quickly. The advances in GPU programming could allow someone with even a few powerful GPUs to break the industry standard of a 1024-bit RSA modulus.

Quantum computing breaks the difficulty for factoring these long RSA numbers. Using the most advanced conventional algorithm, the time it takes to solve these problems grows exponentially with the length of the RSA number. That means by lengthening the RSA number just a little bit, the code becomes drastically harder to break. In 1994, Peter Shor created an algorithm that changes this. The algorithm is known as Shor's algorithm, and the time it takes to solve these problems only grows polynomially with the length of the RSA number. Polynomial time versus exponential time is a huge difference. For example, suppose you are trying to factor a few 100 binary bits. In polynomial time, this would be like multiplying 100 by itself 3 times. This equals one million. Exponential time would be like multiplying 3 by itself 100 times. This roughly equals $5*10^{47}$. These are only approximations to show how different exponential time and polynomial time can be, but they do illustrate how Shor's algorithm is many orders of magnitude more efficient than the best conventional algorithms.

Shor's algorithm is an algorithm only possible on a quantum computer. It uses quantum mechanics to increase the probability of observing the correct answer. A conventional computer can test each possible factorization one at a time. A quantum computer does something drastically different. A quantum computer is like drawing numbers out of a hat. In its most basic state, any given number is just as likely to be drawn as the next. With near infinite possible numbers to draw, and only two being correct, the chances of finding the correct answer are very low. This is when the power of a quantum computer is used. A quantum computer takes the numbers in the hat and floats the correct ones to the top and pushes everything else to the bottom. It makes the correct answer the most likely to be drawn number from the hat. It does this by calculating the period of the number the algorithm is factoring. The period can be used to find the factorization by applying them to the possible solutions. To run this algorithm on a real cryptology algorithm would require a much larger quantum computer

Such a quantum computer does not yet exist. In 2017, IBM unveiled a functioning 50 qubit quantum computer capable of running for 90 microseconds (Knight, 2013). Google unveiled their 72-qubit quantum chip called "Bristlecone" in 2018 (Kelly, 2018). The estimates for breaking an elliptic-curve discrete logarithm problem with a 128-bit security level using a quantum computer would require 2,330 qubits and 126 billion toffoli gates (Roetteler, Naehrig, Svore, & Lauter, 2017). Solving a currently used encryption method would be impossible for one of these systems. The largest number factored using Shor's algorithm was the number 21 (Martín-López, Laing, Lawson, Alvarez, Zhou, & O'Brian, 2012).

While modern quantum computers are not yet capable of using Shor's algorithm to solve any real cryptology algorithms, the potential is certainly there. Shor's algorithm is capable of breaking modern cryptology algorithms in much quicker time than modern algorithms.

A nation with a quantum computer capable of running Shor's algorithm on a powerful quantum computer would leave anyone without a quantum proof algorithm vulnerable. It would make everything connected to the Internet capable of being controlled by international threats. This includes the critical infrastructure that society is built upon. Nations like Russia have already shown their desire and ability to use cyberattacks as a weapon against their enemies. The U.S. infrastructure at best is using encryption methods that are already being obsoleted by non-quantum technologies. When a nation with a powerful quantum computer wants to attack these targets, there would be almost nothing that could be done to prevent this kind of attack. This is a problem that faces not only first world powers capable of developing a quantum computer. This affects everyone with a powergrid and a computer. Low security nations would be liabilities for their allies and should be assisted when it comes to their cyber defense. The United States would be able to assist the defense of poorer countries by providing quantum secure algorithms.

Quantum computers are capable of incredible things. They can access completely different algorithms than conventional computers are able to easily simulate. While development is still slow, there is lots of interest both in the security and research sectors. It will have long reaching implications through the budding field of quantum machine learning. There are also lots of threats posed by a nation acquiring a powerful quantum computer before other nations can defend against one. A nation with a powerful quantum computer would have cyber superiority and be capable of hacking into other nations critical infrastructure. Such a problem could be avoided if powerful nations developed quantum secure algorithms to make such attacks possible to defend against. As with any technology, it is the people that use it that determines if it helps or harms society.

REFERENCES

Cho, A. (2018, January 10). After years of avoidance, Department of Energy joins quest to develop quantum computers. *Science*. Retrieved from www.sciencemag.org/news/2018/01/after-years-avoidance-department-energy-joins-quest-develop-quantum-computers.

Derene, G. (2009, September 30). How vulnerable is U.S. infrastructure to a major cyber attack? *Popular Mechanics*. Retrieved from https://www.popularmechanics.com/military/a4096/4307521/

Gershon, E. (2013, January 14). New qubit control bodes well for future of quantum computing. *Phys.org*. Retrieved from https://phys.org/news/2013-01-qubit-bodes-future-quantum.html.

Kelly, J. (2018, March 5). A preview of Bristlecone, Google's new quantum processor. *Google Research Blog*. Retrieve from https://ai.googleblog.com/2018/03/a-preview-of-bristlecone-googles-new.html

Kleinjung, T., Aoki, K., Franke, J., K. Lenstra, A., Thomé, E., Bos, J., ... Zimmermann, P. (2010). Factorization of a 768-bit RSA modulus. In Rabin, T. (Ed.). *CRYPTO 2010* (pp. 333–350). Santa Barbara, CA: Springer Verlag.

Knight, W. (2013, November 13). IBM announces a trailblazing quantum machine. *MIT Technology Review*. Retrieved from www.technologyreview.com/s/609451/ibm-raises-the-bar-with-a-50-qubit-quantum-computer/.

Lanzagorta, M. & Uhlmann, J.K. (2009). *Quantum Computer Science*. Williston, VT: Morgan & Claypool Publishers.

Martín-López, E., Laing, A., Lawson, T., Alvarez, R., Zhou, Z., & O'Brian, J.L. (2012). Experimental realization of Shor's quantum factoring algorithm using qubit recycling. *Nature Photonics, 6*, 773–776.

Ozhigov, Y. (1999). Quantum computers speed up classical with probability zero. *Chaos, Solitons & Fractals, 10*(10), 1707–1714.

Perlroth, N. & Sanger, D.E. (2018, March 15). Cyberattacks put Russian fingers on the Switch at Power Plants, U.S. says. *The New York Times*. Retrieved from www.nytimes.com/2018/03/15/us/politics/russia-cyberattacks.html.

Roetteler, M., Naehrig, M., Svore, K.M., & Lauter, K. (2017). Quantum resource estimates for computing elliptic curve discrete logarithms. *Microsoft Research, USA*. Retrieved from https://eprint.iacr.org/2017/598.pdf

Sanger, D.E. (2016, February 29). Utilities cautioned about potential for a cyberattack after Ukraine's. *The New York Times*. Retrieved from www.

nytimes.com/2016/03/01/us/politics/utilities-cautioned-about-potential-for-a-cyberattack-after-ukraines.html.

Schuld, M., Sinayskiy, I., & Petruccione, F. (2014). An introduction to quantum learning. *Contemporary Physics, 56*(2), 172–185.

Shor, P.W (1995). Polynomial-time algorithms for prime factorization and discrete logarithms on a quantum computer. *SIAM Journal on Computing, 26,* 1484–1509.

Simonite, T. (2016, February 4). NSA says it "Must Act Now" against the quantum computing threat. *MIT Technology Review.* Retrieved from www.technologyreview.com/s/600715/nsa-says-it-must-act-now-against-the-quantum-computing-threat/.

Strubell, E. (2011). *An introduction to quantum algorithms.* Retrieved from https://people.cs.umass.edu/~strubell/doc/quantum_tutorial.pdf

Waddel, N. (2017, February 6). Quantum computing will revolutionize cancer research, says D-Wave co-founder Farris. *Cantech Letter.* Retrieved March 29, 2018, from https://www.cantechletter.com/2017/02/quantum-computing-will-revolutionize-cancer-research-says-d-wave-co-founder-farris/